Learning to Enjoy the Bible

by

Dan Gallagher

ISBN# 978-0-9628971-8-4
First Edition © 2016

Spirit & Truth Fellowship International®
180 Robert Curry Drive
Martinsville, IN 46151
888.255.6189, M-F 9 to 5
STF@STFonline.org
STFonline.org

Printed in the United States of America.

Table of Contents

Acknowledgments

One of the greatest joys of my life has been the encouragement, inspiration, and insight I have gleaned from reading the Bible. Unfortunately, reading the Bible is for many intimidating, confusing, or a major lesson in frustration. Learning to Enjoy the Bible is my best effort to help those who are seeking to more easily read the Bible, learn from it, and possibly grow closer to the Creator through it.

This book, like most of the other successful endeavors of my life, has been made possible only because of the wonderful team of talented people I work with. Thanks is first due to my wife Lori, from whom I draw much of my strength because of her constant devotion and encouragement. I also owe deep gratitude to my principal editor, Renee Dugan, who not only has provided technical expertise and corrections, but also inspires me daily to write and express myself better. I am also very thankful to John Schoenheit and Jerry Wierwille for their theological reviews and and clarifications. Additionally, this book would never be possible without Janet Speakes' brilliant editing, Ryan Maher's friendship, encouragement, and technical expertise, and Dustin Williams' layout insights and masterful production.

Dedication

Dedicated to my entire family—my parents, Daniel and Betty, and my precious siblings; Bridgit, Molly, Teresa, Margaret, Jack, Kevin, and most especially my special sister Patty. All of whom taught me my first lessons on the meaning of true love, and the importance of family and true friendship.

Introduction

*"It is written, Man does not live by bread
alone, but by every word that proceeds out of
the mouth of God." (Matt. 4:4)*

Most people are surprised to learn that the Bible is the world's #1 bestselling book of all time. Despite the Bible's tremendous popularity and the ageless wisdom it contains, many who pick it up for the first time soon become frustrated with it, primarily because it is not like most other books they read. Normally we have an immediate sense of the story or theme that a book is going to portray; in the case of a novel, we start in chapter one and watch the plot unfold as the characters and storylines develop.

It's not that the Bible doesn't have a theme—it does! The overarching story of the Bible is told through the records of hundreds of colorful characters—real people with real life-sized problems, trials, and victories. The message of the Bible unfolds through its many dramatic stories and truly epic tales. There is most definitely a divine purpose portrayed through its pages, and it's of vital importance for all mankind.

So with all this in its favor, why is it that some still find the Bible hard to read and understand? It's a fair question, and the answer involves a number of factors that this book will address. Perhaps you are reading this book because you are one of many who struggle to read the Bible. The purpose of this short book is to help you avoid frustration and confusion, and to connect you to the theme of the Bible so that you can "learn to enjoy the Bible." Then hopefully you, like millions of others, will be able to gain inspiration, enlightenment, and a deeper spiritual relationship with its Author.

Learning to Enjoy the Bible

by

Dan Gallagher

ISBN# 978-0-9628971-8-4
First Edition © 2016

Spirit & Truth Fellowship International®
180 Robert Curry Drive
Martinsville, IN 46151
888.255.6189, M-F 9 to 5
STF@STFonline.org
STFonline.org

Printed in the United States of America.

Table of Contents

Acknowledgments

One of the greatest joys of my life has been the encouragement, inspiration, and insight I have gleaned from reading the Bible. Unfortunately, reading the Bible is for many intimidating, confusing, or a major lesson in frustration. Learning to Enjoy the Bible is my best effort to help those who are seeking to more easily read the Bible, learn from it, and possibly grow closer to the Creator through it.

This book, like most of the other successful endeavors of my life, has been made possible only because of the wonderful team of talented people I work with. Thanks is first due to my wife Lori, from whom I draw much of my strength because of her constant devotion and encouragement. I also owe deep gratitude to my principal editor, Renee Dugan, who not only has provided technical expertise and corrections, but also inspires me daily to write and express myself better. I am also very thankful to John Schoenheit and Jerry Wierwille for their theological reviews and and clarifications. Additionally, this book would never be possible without Janet Speakes' brilliant editing, Ryan Maher's friendship, encouragement, and technical expertise, and Dustin Williams' layout insights and masterful production.

Dedication

Dedicated to my entire family—my parents, Daniel and Betty, and my precious siblings; Bridgit, Molly, Teresa, Margaret, Jack, Kevin, and most especially my special sister Patty. All of whom taught me my first lessons on the meaning of true love, and the importance of family and true friendship.

Introduction

*"It is written, Man does not live by bread
alone, but by every word that proceeds out of
the mouth of God." (Matt. 4:4)*

Most people are surprised to learn that the Bible is the world's #1 bestselling book of all time. Despite the Bible's tremendous popularity and the ageless wisdom it contains, many who pick it up for the first time soon become frustrated with it, primarily because it is not like most other books they read. Normally we have an immediate sense of the story or theme that a book is going to portray; in the case of a novel, we start in chapter one and watch the plot unfold as the characters and storylines develop.

It's not that the Bible doesn't have a theme—it does! The overarching story of the Bible is told through the records of hundreds of colorful characters—real people with real life-sized problems, trials, and victories. The message of the Bible unfolds through its many dramatic stories and truly epic tales. There is most definitely a divine purpose portrayed through its pages, and it's of vital importance for all mankind.

So with all this in its favor, why is it that some still find the Bible hard to read and understand? It's a fair question, and the answer involves a number of factors that this book will address. Perhaps you are reading this book because you are one of many who struggle to read the Bible. The purpose of this short book is to help you avoid frustration and confusion, and to connect you to the theme of the Bible so that you can "learn to enjoy the Bible." Then hopefully you, like millions of others, will be able to gain inspiration, enlightenment, and a deeper spiritual relationship with its Author.

Part One:
What is it?

1

Why Read the Bible?

Over the years, I've watched with amazement as my wife has patiently transformed jumbled piles of jigsaw puzzle pieces into beautiful pictures. She inherited her love of puzzles from her mom; I, on the other hand...well, I've always struggled with them, partly because of my red-green colorblindness (or at least that's the excuse I like to use). As I've watched over her shoulder, I've realized there are some clear strategies that successful puzzlers use.

Learning to enjoy the Bible is in many ways like learning how to put together the pieces of a jigsaw puzzle; there are proper methodologies that can keep us from getting lost in the pieces. In the same way that a puzzle's individual pieces are part of a much bigger picture, the individual verses and separate sections of the Bible need to be properly joined together so that we can see the full picture.

Can you imagine how hard it would be to put together a jigsaw puzzle if you had no idea what the completed picture was supposed to look like? Thankfully, every jigsaw puzzle comes with a clear picture on the top of the box, which every successful puzzle maker knows is the most important reference tool. Similarly, the overarching message of the Bible is a picture that we must know in order to properly fit together the various characters, stories, poems, prophetic references, and more.

When we open a puzzle box and dump all the contents out on the table, we are faced with a disjointed, jumbled mess. The best way to approach this pile of pieces is to have a strategy, a systematic way of sorting them before we even begin to fit them together. Most puzzlers know that you start with the edge and corner pieces, the borders of the picture, which then serve as the framework in which the rest of the pieces come together. It is also helpful to sort pieces that make up the subthemes—pictures or shapes

> **A big step in learning to enjoy the Bible lies in developing an understanding of how to fit the pieces together...**

within the overall picture, like the cows, ducks, horses, and chickens that are part of a puzzle of a farm. With both the Bible and a puzzle, as we begin to understand the subthemes and how they all fit properly together, we then begin to see the beauty of the picture they portray.

Unfortunately, many people become frustrated when they first attempt to read the Bible because they don't really have a clear sense about the picture on the box, so to speak. A big step in learning to enjoy the Bible lies in developing an understanding of how to fit the pieces together, and as we do this we will see a masterpiece unfold before our eyes. But before we get into deeper discussion on the particulars of the Bible, let's first lay the foundation of why we should even bother learning to enjoy the Bible.

Why Read the Bible?

Most all religions have some form of a sacred text; Hinduism has the Shruti, Islam has the Qur'an, Mormonism has the Book of Mormon, and so on. The Bible is the Holy Book of Christianity, and besides being the #1 bestselling book of all time, it has been a source of inspiration and strength for millions of people throughout the ages.

For the Christian, the Bible is considered to be God's instructions for mankind regarding how to live rightly. It's a source of wisdom concerning relationships, money, parenting, and other matters of fruitful living. Many have reported that regularly reading the Bible has provided them a sense of peace, clarity, and direction for their lives. One thing that reading the Bible makes clear is that there is a right way and a wrong way to live. It's filled with stories of real people, some who did good and some who suffered the consequences of doing wrong. One benefit of reading the Bible is that we can learn from the mistakes and successes of others, and then apply those lessons directly to ourselves and our life situations.

The Bible says that within its pages God has given us everything that we need in order to live the way He intends us to. It also says that the words it contains were recorded by men as God instructed them. This is why the Bible declares itself to be the "Word of God."

A Jewish king named David recorded one of the main reasons why we should desire to read and understand the Bible. He said, "I have hidden your word in my heart so that I might not sin against you" (Psalm 119:11). If we truly want to grow closer to God, understand what He wants for us, and know how best to live lives that are pleasing to Him, we need to know His instructions; and just as King David said, knowing God's Word helps us to do that. The Bible gives people instruction, encouragement, peace, and inner strength, and learning to enjoy it can change your life. The famous Christian author A.W. Tozer wrote:

"The Word of God, well understood and religiously obeyed, is the shortest route to spiritual perfection. And we must not select a few favorite passages to the exclusion of others. Nothing less than a whole Bible can make a whole Christian."

2

Understanding the
Background of the Bible

The Bible — The World's "Best Seller"

The Bible is the greatest publishing success of all time. It was the first book that came off the printing press invented by Johannes Gutenberg in 1440. It's amazing to think that this one book has been translated into more languages (about 350 at last count) and has sold more copies than any other book in all of history (about 100 million annually).

The Bible Can Be Intimidating and Frustrating

In spite of the Bible's great popularity, many who read it for the first time end up somewhat confused and frustrated. The sheer size of the Bible, with its approximately two thousand pages, can leave the novice reader feeling quite intimidated. However, most who read the Bible on a regular basis claim that it's like no other book that they have read, leaving them with a sense of awe, inspiration, and spiritual enlightenment.

Oftentimes the problem first-time readers encounter stems from a misunderstanding of the Bible's nature, purpose, origin, authorship, and composition. Understandably, many attempt to read it like they would a novel, where one becomes immersed in the storyline as the plot develops through interactions between the major and minor characters. The problem with approaching the Bible this way is that it simply doesn't work—it isn't a novel!

Taking the time to learn the Bible's background and nature will go a long way toward enhancing the experience of reading it, and will greatly aid us in avoiding confusion and frustration.

Why is the Bible Called "The Bible?"

One of the first questions many people have about the Bible is, "What does the word Bible mean?" "Bible" comes from the Latin word biblia and the Greek word biblios, both of which mean "book" or "scroll." Books as we know them today, with many individual pages bound together in one text, didn't exist in the ancient world. People wrote on rolls of animal skins or plant material (called papyrus), and these rolls were often sewed together, in which case they became fairly long.

Byblos, an ancient city located in what's now Lebanon, was famous for the valuable papyrus reed scrolls made there. These "paper" scrolls were used throughout the ancient world, and eventually the name "Byblos" became synonymous with the papyrus scrolls that were produced there. This is similar to how nowadays people often refer to any small adhesive bandage as a Band-Aid, despite the fact that Band-Aid© is the official brand name of one particular product.

Nowadays, we still see the original sense of "Bible" retained in the Spanish language with its use of "biblioteca," meaning a library—a place where many books are kept. In English we also use "bibliography," which is a list of the various books an author cites as reference sources. Thus, the word "Bible" simply means "book." As you progress in your knowledge of its contents, you will likely discover, as many others have, that it's truly "The Book" of the ages.

The Bible's Role in the History of Writing

Although we have the benefit of reading our modern Bible as a single book, this present form is actually a relatively recent development. The fact that it is a single volume is somewhat misleading because it wasn't originally produced this way; instead it is a compilation of many individual writings.

> One of the central tenets of the Bible is that, although there were 40 different writers, God was the single Author because He was the one who inspired the words those people wrote.

Today we live in a highly literate world, but throughout the majority of human history this hasn't been the case. The advancement of writing was a huge turning point for mankind, and the Bible is right at the epicenter of the development of writing, especially in the use of an alphabet instead of picture-writing. As writing first developed, it was practiced primarily by an elite few. The entire writing process was a fairly costly endeavor, with the great price of the parchment—whether papyrus or animal hide, which required a very time-consuming process to make—as well as the time required to dictate and the cost of a professional scribe to write the information down. The high costs involved meant that writing wasn't a frivolous matter, so, for the most part, what was written was considered enormously important.

The ability to retain information in written form in very ancient times was highly valued by rulers and religious leaders, as it aided their ability to transmit information accurately, even from one generation to the next. The great regard placed upon these scrolls meant that they were safeguarded, even treasured by many, depending upon the nature and authorship of the contents.

The Bible's Diverse Background
The Bible is a compilation of many scrolls from 40 different writers written over a period of more than 1,500 years. These writers varied widely in their cultural backgrounds, historical settings, and occupations, which included shepherds, nobility, prophets, priests, and laymen. The content they wrote was equally diverse, covering religious practices, morals and ethics, history, poetry, music, personal letters, and prophecy. When we consider all of these factors, it helps us to understand the range of the writing styles, stories, and other information contained in the Bible.

The Uniqueness of the Bible
One of the central tenets of the Bible is that, although there were 40 different writers, God was the single Author

because He was the one who inspired the words those people wrote. Another very unique aspect of the Bible is that despite there being so many different writers whose works encompassed more than a 1,500 year period, it remains a cohesive story about the plans and purposes of God for mankind and His moves throughout history to bring those plans about.

...the Bible is a book that depicts the good, the bad, and the ugly of mankind as the stories reveal triumph and failure, faithfulness and futility.

As a "religious book," another exceptional feature of the Bible is that many of the characters it describes are far from "perfect." In fact, there is a great moral diversity in the stories. Even within the first pages of the Bible we read about disobedience, family breakdowns, murder, and rebellion. It can be said that the Bible is a book that depicts the good, the bad, and the ugly of mankind as the stories reveal triumph and failure, faithfulness and futility. One thing that makes the Bible so believable—and so easy to relate to—is the writers' refusal to sugarcoat the characters and their human frailty. God includes adulterers, embezzlers, traitors, and villains as well as the meek, strong, honorable, and victorious in telling the story of mankind—and sometimes these good and bad traits are present in the same person! This is clearly a book that covers the whole gamut of human emotion from utter despair to joyous elation.

3

The Bible as a Work
of Literature

There are many different genres of books, such as fiction, autobiographical, scientific, and poetic, and the way we read each type varies. In the case of a novel, we begin reading on page one and proceed from the front of the book to the back. The plot develops as the story progresses with characters entering and exiting and the central conflict resolving in the novel's climax. This is quite different from a dictionary, encyclopedia, or technical manual. The last thing we would do with those is start in the beginning and then read until we come to the word or information we need. Everyone understands that the way we approach a book depends upon the kind of book it is.

The Bible is no different. Learning to enjoy it requires that we understand it as a collection of many different genres, each serving a different purpose. Besides the many stories of people and events, it also contains poetry, prophetic warnings and sayings, proverbs, letters, and more. Since the Bible also served the Jewish nation as a historical and legal record, it includes genealogical lists, census records, and religious, sacrificial, and legal instructions. The Bible is a very diverse compilation of widely-ranging materials, some which have direct bearing on us today and some which don't; nevertheless, there are great truths and insights that everyone can glean from it.

> **Many critics of the Bible consider its stories to be fables, but there is solid historical and archeological evidence to indicate that they are about real people, times, places, and events.**

For clarity's sake, let's look at the various kinds of literature in the Bible:

Narrative

A narrative is a story, and the Bible certainly has plenty of those. In fact, many of the stories in the Bible are very famous, such as the accounts of Adam and Eve, Noah, Moses, and of course, Jesus. The Bible even begins with the account of creation, a story that opens with the words, "In the beginning God created the heavens and the earth." As we progress through the Bible, we read the stories of various men and women God has worked with throughout history in pursuit of His plans and purposes. Eventually we come to the story of Jesus—his life, death, and resurrection—followed by the book of Acts, which is a story about the very first followers of Jesus Christ, their ups and downs, and the spread of Jesus' message by them throughout the Roman Empire. Lastly, the Bible closes with the Book of Revelation and its portrayal of the story of the end times and man's final reunion and life with God.

Many critics of the Bible consider its stories to be fables, but there is solid historical and archeological evidence to indicate that they are about real people, times, places, and events. Some of the beauty of the biblical narrative lies in the fact that it depicts people experiencing genuine struggles that most of us can relate to.

We also need to keep in mind that these are stories from ancient times and that, although they involve some very different cultures and customs, they also include relevant lessons of moral, ethical, and religious principles that can guide us all. It can rightly be said that the stories in the Bible are about the whole human condition, the moral and the immoral, the good and the bad. This isn't a storybook of perfect characters with perfect lives, but of real people with blemishes, warts, and all. When the narratives are threaded together, they depict the overall story of God's love for mankind, His desire for the relationship between mankind and Himself to be restored, and what He has done to bring that to pass.

Here are some examples of the various stories in the Bible:

- The Creation of the world and mankind (Genesis 1-2)
- The Fall of Man—his disobedience (Genesis 3)

- Noah and the flood (Genesis 6-8)
- Abraham and the promise God made to him (Genesis 12-23)
- Joseph sold into slavery, and his rise to power inEgypt (Genesis 37-50)
- Moses—his birth, calling, confrontation with Pharaoh, and the Exodus (Exodus 1-20; 32-35)
- The Israelites wandering in the desert (Numbers 11-17; 20-25)
- Joshua conquering the Promised Land (Joshua 1-11; 22-24)
- The various judges of Israel (Judges 1-21)
- Kings Saul, David, and Solomon (1 & 2 Samuel; 1 Kings 1-11; 1 Chronicles 10-29; 2 Chronicles 1-9)
- The Israelite captivity in Assyria and Babylon (2 Kings 17-25)
- Jesus—his birth, life, death, and resurrection (Matthew, Mark, Luke, John)
- The first-century followers (Acts)
- The End Times and the Final Kingdom (Revelation 6-22)

Prophecy

Most people think of prophecies as predictions concerning future events, and although this is true, prophecy can also involve God's instruction for people to "Get moving!", or to stop doing something that is harmful. For the most part, the biblical writers were prophets to whom God revealed His instructions, corrections, and words of encouragement.

Early in the Book of Genesis, the first book of the Bible, there is a story of a man named Abraham and his wife, Sarah. The Bible records how, almost two thousand years after Adam disobeyed God, He chose Abraham and promised him that he would be "the Father of many nations" and that through him all the people of the world would be blessed. This was a prophecy regarding the future coming of a Messiah, a special man appointed by God to help restore the relationship that Adam had broken. There are many sections of the Bible that contain prophetic words

> As we gain a better understanding of the characters and storylines of the Bible, we will be better able to enjoy the prophetic sections...

pertaining to the Messiah and the Nation of Israel that came from Abraham's descendants.

Oftentimes prophecies can be hard to understand because of their obscured and enigmatic nature. God spoke to prophets using pictures and riddles, which can be confusing, so generally when first learning to enjoy the Bible the reader may want to skim, or even jump over, some prophetic sections. As we gain a better understanding of the characters and storylines of the Bible, we will be better able to enjoy the prophetic sections and the rich truths they reveal about God's plans and actions throughout history.

Prophetic sections are embedded throughout the Bible, but some of them include:

- Isaiah (Chapters 1-66)
- Jeremiah (Chapters 1-38; 44-51)
- Ezekiel (Chapters 1-48)
- Daniel (Chapters 2; 4; 5;7-12)

Wisdom
One of the things that the Bible declares about itself is that it holds instruction on fruitful living. It describes wisdom as knowing the right, fair, and just path, and it includes some wonderfully inspiring sections about the meaning of life,

relational skills, and practical keys to being the best person possible.

Many people make it a daily habit to read from the Book of Proverbs or Ecclesiastes because of the great wisdom these sections contain. Sprinkled throughout the Bible are pithy sayings and tidbits of wisdom spoken by many godly men and women which, when allowed to sink into our hearts, can eventually be incorporated into our lives as well.

Some of the wisdom sections include:

- Job (Chapters 3-42)
- Psalms
- Proverbs
- Ecclesiastes

Poetry

About the most profound poetry I've ever personally written has started off with the words, "Roses are red, violets are blue," so clearly I am not much of an expert on poetry. When reading the biblical sections that contain poetry, we should keep in mind that it's an Eastern book, originally written in other languages for people with other cultures, customs and practices. The poetry sections found in the Old Testament were originally written in Hebrew, so, like all translations from one language to another, the poetic words and concepts don't necessarily translate perfectly into English.

We should also be aware that many of the psalms were intended to be sung as lyrics in musical praise with instrumental accompaniment. Although the English reader may not recognize all the poetic nuances, most will find these sections to be very inspirational, and enriching in their praise life toward God.

The poetic sections include:

- Job
- Psalms
- Song of Solomon
- Lamentations

Correspondence

There are many letters recorded in the Bible, especially in the New Testament. Of the 27 books in the New Testament, 21 were originally written as letters to individuals or to entire congregations of the first followers of Jesus. The Bible has many records of letters, and even the Book of Revelation, which speaks of many events still to come in the future, contains seven letters written to seven churches. In the Old Testament as well, the reader

> **The New Testament letters are very valuable for learning the instructions of the Apostles on how Christians are to think, believe, and act.**

will find the occasional letter from a king to his subjects, royal decrees, announcements, etc.

The New Testament letters are very valuable for learning the instructions of the Apostles on how Christians are to think, believe, and act. Although the letters were written in the first century, they still have direct relevance to all Christians today. Every follower of Jesus should take the time to read the New Testament letters, also known as the Epistles, in order to understand the fundamentals of the Christian faith.

Letters normally include an opening salutation, the identity of the author, the intended audience, prayers, instructions, wisdom, warnings, quotations from the Old Testament prophets, and even personal news. It's also noteworthy that, unlike the Old Testament which was originally written in Hebrew, the New Testament letters were penned in Greek, since it was the universal language of commerce and trade and was therefore spoken throughout the entire Roman Empire.

Examples of correspondence include:

- Romans
- 1 and 2 Corinthians
- Galatians
- Ephesians
- Philippians
- Colossians
- 1 and 2 Thessalonians
- 1 and 2 Timothy
- Titus
- Philemon
- Hebrews*
- James
- 1 and 2 Peter
- 1, 2, and 3 John
- Jude

*Many scholars consider Hebrews to be a combination of genres that is not purely fitting within the category of a letter. It is included in this list because it is commonly included in the list of the Epistles.

Religious Instruction

In the Old Testament we are told how God worked through Abraham's offspring to raise up a special nation through which He would bring the Messiah—the anointed one of God who would save the entire world. Later God called Moses, a special prophet, to lead the Nation of Israel out from their Egyptian slavery. God needed to keep the people separate from other nations, both religiously and socially, so

He instituted religious, dietary, clothing, and special social regulations through Moses, who in turn instructed the people in them.

These regulations can be tedious to read, and even the seasoned Bible reader tends to skip over many of them since they seem to be repetitive. The reader should always bear in mind that God had a specific reason for these instructions and that there is much we can glean from them, but when first learning how to enjoy the Bible, we don't need to get bogged down by them. For this reason, I encourage first-time Bible readers to skim these sections and just get a feel for them and what was required of the Nation of Israel thousands of years ago; this will help the reader, when approaching the New Testament, to still appreciate how these regulations have changed as a result of the perfect sacrifice of Christ, without getting weighed down or confused.

These special rules and regulations given to Israel are mainly recorded in:

- Exodus
- Leviticus
- Numbers
- Deuteronomy

Legal and Genealogical Records

In western societies, religious and civil or governmental institutions are separate, but in Israel the government was a combination of both the civil and the religious. There are times when the reader will encounter sections that speak about behavior from both perspectives. There are also a number of records that list the genealogies of people—that is, who is the father of whom. Although it's easy to get lost in the lists of names, these were very important records that were used to establish priestly credentials and to ultimately validate the Messiah in light of his genealogy. The reader will find genealogical lists sprinkled throughout the Bible.

Having a good grasp of the type of literature we're encountering in any given section will go a long way toward helping us learn to enjoy the Bible. If you find a section that is confusing or even boring, just skip over it. You can always come back to it at a later time. As you develop a stronger feel for the plans and actions of God, you will be able to better comprehend the difficult sections and gain greater appreciation for what God has done—and is still doing!

4

Why is the Bible Considered a Holy Book?

I was nineteen years old when I first began to read the Bible, and at that time the most popular version was the King James Bible. It was originally compiled in 1611 AD and uses terms like "thee" and "thou," "whilst" and "doth," just like people did in Shakespeare's time. But let's face it—we don't talk that way nowadays because it's archaic, and that means that versions like the King James Version can be hard for the modern reader to understand. Although many people eventually get used to it, there are many easier-to-read versions available now, so I don't recommend that the first-time Bible reader use a King James Bible. It may have worked for King James and Shakespeare, but the way it reads will confuse most people today.

When picking up the King James Bible, you will also notice that right on the cover it says "Holy Bible," a phrase that was used for the first time on that version. Although many other versions nowadays merely say "The Bible," the belief that it's the "Holy Book" remains for Christians today.

Why is the Bible Considered to Be a Holy Book?

Why do most Christians believe the Bible is a Holy Book—and what does that even mean? The words of all the biblical writers were considered very special by the people they wrote to because the people believed that the writers were delivering the words of God. This understanding is based on God being "holy," meaning that He is separate and apart from us because of His sacredness, purity, and perfect nature. Furthermore, there are numerous places where the Bible actually says that God is holy. Here are a few that are familiar to most Bible readers:

1 Samuel 2:2 (NIV)
"There is no one holy like the LORD; there is no one besides you;

Psalm 99:9 (NIV)
Exalt the LORD our God and worship at his holy mountain, for the LORD our God is holy.

Revelation 4:8 (NIV)
Each of the four living creatures had six wings and

was covered with eyes all around, even under its wings. Day and night they never stop saying: "Holy, holy, holy is the Lord God Almighty, who was, and is, and is to come."

The reason that the Bible is considered "holy" is because God is a holy God, and that means His words are holy, too.

How Did We Get the Bible?

The Bible is a compilation of 66 individual books written by numerous writers over more than a 1,500 year period. I specifically use the phrase "written by" because most Christians recognize that although there were many writers, there was one Author—God. Through the ages, men recorded what God directed them to, so in a sense the writers were God's secretaries recording what He inspired them to write.

There are numerous places where God instructed Moses to record His words and then to instruct the people. Contained within the books of Moses—the first five books of the Bible—are detailed instructions for Israel, covering a wide range of topics including the Ten Commandments, the construction of the Tabernacle, sacrificial practices, the Feasts of Israel, and more. In some instances, such as with Moses, God directly dictated the words. At other times He inspired His prophets what to write through His spirit. Essentially, no matter how God did it, the words in the Bible are understood to be His words.

Inspired by God—Men Wrote as God Directed

This principle of how men were given the words to write is revealed in the Bible itself where it says, "All Scripture is God-breathed..." (2 Timothy 3:16 NIV). The phrase "God-breathed" is translated from the Greek word, theopneustos, which is a compound word comprised of Theos (God) and pneustos (breathed).

Whenever we speak, we do so by exhaling air as we form and enunciate syllables. But before we can exhale the air to speak, we must first inhale air—draw it into our lungs. When the Bible says that "all Scripture is God-breathed," or "inspired by God," it means the writers received the words like air from God, and exhaled them as they spoke. This understanding is further expressed in 2 Peter:

2 Peter 1:20-21 (NIV)
(20) Above all, you must understand that no prophecy of Scripture came about by the prophet's own interpretation of things.
(21) For prophecy [words from God] never had its origin in the human will, but prophets, though human, spoke from God as they were carried along by the Holy Spirit.

Peter is clear that the words did not originate in man; they originated in the mind of God, and the prophets spoke and wrote as God inspired them.

Who is the Bible Intended For?

There has never been any shortage of critics of the Bible. Some say it's full of myths or that you can't trust it. Most who criticize it do so from the "outside," so to speak—they are scoffers and unbelievers. But who exactly is the Bible written for? Is the purpose of the Bible to convince the skeptics that God really does exist?

The Bible makes it clear that God's words aren't intended to convince the doubters, but instead are for the "servant of God." The servant of God is anyone who desires to "serve" God and live in a way that is pleasing to Him, doing His will and remaining obedient to His decrees. These are spiritual words directed toward those who desire spiritual food and seek to love and serve God; to do that, they must know His desires and instructions. The Bible was never directed toward the unbeliever and those who reject God.

Before his death, my father gave me a treasured family heirloom—a special ring. The last thing I would ever do is treat it disrespectfully, such as tossing it into the mud and stepping on it. If my father had had any inkling that I was going to treat his priceless heirloom like that, he would have never given it to me in the first place. Instead, he would have passed it on to someone he knew would respect and treat it as the valuable object it is. In a similar way, God's Word is very precious, worth more than silver or gold, and He doesn't entrust it to anyone who holds contempt for Him.

> **True biblical faith isn't a mystical or metaphysical mindset or a belief in something for which there is no proof.**

Hebrews 11:6 (NIV)
And without faith [trust] it's impossible to please God, because anyone who comes to him must believe that he exists and that he rewards those who earnestly seek him.

The entire testimony of the Bible is that God works with those who seek and trust Him. True biblical faith isn't a mystical or metaphysical mindset or a belief in something for which there is no proof. We have genuine faith in God when we trust Him and are confident that He will do what He says He will. Throughout human history God has rewarded those who seek Him, trust Him, and obey Him. Chapter 11 of the Book of Hebrews wonderfully demonstrates this principle when it lists and describes many heroes of faith:

Hebrews 11:7, 8, 23
(7) "By faith Noah, when warned...condemned the world and became the heir of righteousness...
(8) By faith Abraham, when called...obeyed...
(23) By faith, Moses' parents hid him..."

God's words were delivered to men and women who trusted Him and strived to obey Him. These are the kinds of people for whom the Bible is intended.

What is the Purpose of the Bible?

There are a number of purposes for the individual books in the Bible, but overall the Bible serves as a guide to those who desire to love and serve God. By understanding God's desires for mankind, as well as His ways, we learn how to obey and please Him.

Psalm 119:9-11 (NIV)
(9) How can a young person stay on the path of purity?
By living according to your word.
(10) I seek you with all my heart; do not let me stray from your commands.
(11) I have hidden your word in my heart that I might not sin against you.

Previously we learned that the scriptures are God-breathed—they are words inspired by God (2 Timothy 3:16). In this same passage, in addition to learning how the words came to man, we also learn who they were intended for and what their purpose is. Let's look at the whole verse as quoted below:

2 Timothy 3:16-17 (NIV)
(16) All Scripture is God-breathed and is useful for teaching, rebuking, correcting and training in righteousness,

(17) so that the servant of God may be thoroughly equipped for every good work.

Teaching is instruction concerning God's plans, purposes, and actions throughout history, as well as the right things to think and do in life. It's the "what" and "how" of living right. Unfortunately, we all stumble, so when we do, rebuking brings our missteps to our attention and points out our error. Once we become aware of that error, correction shows us how to get back on the right path. When we put the teaching, rebuking, and correction together, they become a package that provides us "training in righteousness"—right living. This is one of the purposes of the Bible.

> **When we put the teaching, rebuking, and correction together, they become a package that provides us "training in righteousness"**

The Words of God Are Pure

Unlike the words that we speak, the holy nature of God results in His words always being true and pure. The Psalmist paints a vivid picture of the purity of God's words when he compares them to silver in the refiner's furnace.

Psalm 12:6 (NIV)
And the words of the LORD are flawless, like silver purified in a crucible, like gold refined seven times.

Refining is the process used to remove the impurities from precious metals like gold and silver. One method used to purify the metal is to heat it in a crucible until it liquefies, which causes the dross—the impurities—to float to the top, where they can be removed. Normally this would be done two or three times to achieve a very high purity.

In the case of God's words, He says they are as pure as silver or gold refined up to seven times. This means they are completely pure, perfectly flawless, without any contaminates. Many times when the number seven is used in the Bible, it signifies that something is spiritually perfect. In this case, with the comparison between God's Word and precious metals refined seven times, God is telling us that we can trust His words because they are absolutely flawless—spiritually perfect.

Here are a few other references to God's words to consider:

Psalm 19:9-10 (NIV)
(9) The decrees of the LORD are firm, and all of them are righteous.
(10) They are more precious than gold, than much pure gold; they are sweeter than honey, than honey from the honeycomb.

Psalm 119:160 (NIV)
All your words are true; all your righteous laws are eternal.

Psalm 119:43 (NIV)
Never take your word of truth from my mouth, for I have put my hope in your laws.

John 17:17 (NIV)
Sanctify them by the truth; your word is truth.

What Evidence is There that God Inspired the Words in the Bible?

This is a very important question because if there is no evidence to support the claim that the Bible is in fact God's Word, then we only have people's opinions and no real reason to trust it. Listed below are some of the reasons why we can trust the Bible.

1. Archeological Evidence

Occasionally we hear people say that there is no archeological evidence for the Flood of Noah, the Exodus of the Israelites from Egypt, or other biblical events. But in actuality there is a tremendous amount of archeological evidence that confirms many biblical accounts, and new discoveries of additional physical evidence are being made on a regular basis.

Archeological studies have now confirmed the reigns of biblical kings mentioned in the books of 1 and 2 Kings, such as Omri, Ahab, Uzziah, Hezzekiah, Jeroboam II, and Jehoiachin. The ancient city of Lachish has been discovered and the accounts of it in the Bible match its physical location and the Assyrian siege against it (2 Kings 18-19). One of the most famous discoveries of the 20th century was the Dead Sea Scrolls, a large volume of scrolls hidden in caves in the area of the Dead Sea, which corroborated the reliability of many Old Testament texts. There have also been innumerable discoveries of artifacts, cities, and edifices that confirm the reigns of Kings David and Solomon, the existence of the Temple, and much more.

...just because we haven't discovered evidence for some of the people, places, or things in the Bible doesn't mean they didn't exist.

One of the flaws of archeology is that, although scientists may agree on the discovery of artifacts and their locations, they often disagree on the timeframes in which they were made or the significance of the items themselves. The critics once said that there was no evidence for a Hittite empire as described in the Bible—that is, until the day when scholars discovered the remains of the Hittite empire exactly where the Bible described it! We must bear in mind that just because we haven't discovered evidence for some of the people, places, or things in the Bible doesn't mean they didn't exist. It simply means we haven't found the evidence yet, or possibly that archeologists have misidentified what they've already found. Today there are many books that provide ample archeological evidence for the validity of the Bible.

2. Textual Consistency

One principle argument people use to attack the validity of the Bible is to say that the text cannot be trusted. Sometimes they claim, "It has been copied so many times that there is no way we can prove it's still accurate." Although on the surface this argument may seem to have some merit, the facts actually don't support it.

When determining the validity of a manuscript, scholars rely on the number of copies that exist and the proximity in time of the manuscript's copies to the original. When it comes to the Bible, the volume of textual evidence is overwhelming. There are now over 5,700 copies of the Greek text consisting of over 2.5 million pages of text, and the amount of material is increasing each year as new discoveries are made. In addition to the early copies, we also have a large number of quotations of the Bible in the writings of the early church fathers. Today, with the aid of modern computers, we can actually develop a very accurate rendering of the original text.

Scholars who work with ancient manuscripts commonly recognize that the more copies that exist, the greater the possibility of reconstructing the original document. The ability to compare the various texts allows the textual researcher to fill in any missing sections and to identify any additions that may have been made. Scholars are even so convinced of the completeness of the biblical textual record that they now commonly place its purity at 99.5%.

3. Literary Consistency

Another point that speaks to God's genuine authorship of the Bible is the consistency of the writing. It's amazing that despite its 66 books being written by 40 people who wrote over more than a 1,500-year span, the Bible still has a clear literary consistency. These were writers who lived in many different countries, with differing cultures, writing in different languages and in many different genres, and yet there is a single unifying theme—one story which flows from beginning to end, culminating in the accomplishment of God's plans and purposes. When we consider how rare it is to get even a handful of eyewitnesses to agree on a simple event that they have all personally witnessed, the thematic unity of the Bible is incredible. This amazing thematic unity points directly to a single author—God!

4. Prophetic Proof

Additional proof of the divine authorship of the Bible is the historically verifiable prophecies that it contains. One of the most interesting aspects of the Bible is that it contains a lot of predictive prophecy—the foretelling of events before they happened. In fact, a significant portion of the Old Testament is predictive, possibly as much as 25-30%. In particular, it's very noteworthy that, with the exception of those things concerning Jesus' second coming in the future and the end times, he fulfilled every single one of the 300-plus prophecies about the Messiah. At times, people may be able to make somewhat good predictions about the future, but never to the degree and accuracy of the prophetic sections in the Bible. This prophetic evidence indicates a supernatural force at work.

Why So Many Bible Translations?

Walk into any modern Christian bookstore to purchase a Bible, and you will probably be overwhelmed by how many translations there are to choose from. There are actually over 100 English translations of the Bible, and they all vary to some degree. What we need to keep in mind is that there was only one original text that was written, and it's not the original text that varies, but the translations of that text.

The Old Testament was written in Hebrew and the New Testament in Greek. Whenever a document is translated from one language into another, the translator must choose which word best fits the author's message. Although it may seem simple to choose an English word when translating from Greek or Hebrew, this isn't always the case. Languages reflect cultures and the way people think, which means there may be times when there isn't an English word that perfectly conveys the original concept. The translator must then make a judgment call on how to convey the meaning—and, of course, translators may disagree on the choices made.

> ...no matter what translation you choose, the Bible is the Word of God, and as such it has the power to transform your life...

There are other times when a word can have a wide range of meanings, and the translator must choose from a pool of words. For instance, in Greek we may have a word that means "to touch someone", and the translator must decide which of the following words fits best: brush, tap, bump, hit, slap, push, pull, knock, slam, etc. As you can see, all of these English words are a form of "touching" another person, but they each convey a very different concept, so the word the translator chooses can greatly alter the meaning. Translators determine the correct word to use based on the context of the section, but personal biases and understandings affect all translations.

Another reason there are so many English translations is because languages change over time. The King James Version was originally translated in 1611, and what a word meant at the time of Shakespeare often means something very different today. Languages are fluid; the meanings of words change as society and cultures change, which is why various translations can eventually become "out of date."

After reading the Bible for many years, I now tend to read a number of different translations when studying, but for personal enjoyment I prefer to read for pleasure a version that I have grown accustomed to. When first learning to enjoy the Bible, choose a translation that is easy for you to read and understand, and remember: no matter what translation you choose, the Bible is the Word of God, and as such it has the power to transform your life as He speaks to you through it.

Part Two:
What Does It All Mean?

5

Developing a Proper Understanding

Have you ever been so busy that instead of taking the time to call and speak directly to a coworker or friend, you sent off a short reply in an email or text message—but then your brief message was misunderstood and even caused the other person to be offended? The message may have been accurate, but your brevity came at a high price because the other person mistook it for anger or condescension and may have even misinterpreted your words.

Most of us can relate to relationship breakdowns resulting from miscommunications, especially ones that involve written messages. Even if the words are carefully crafted, accurately chosen, and properly ordered, written communication can still have some serious limitations. Like a pathway with potholes and snags, the minute we rely on letter-writing instead of face-to-face communication, we begin a journey that has the potential of tripping us up.

Communication involves much more than the mere transfer of words between people. Words are only one part of communication. Speaking directly to another person is the clearest and safest form of communication because we are able to hear the other person's tone of voice and pay attention to the way words are enunciated as we watch their body language and facial gestures. This helps us to determine the emotional content of the message, which is a very large part of communication. A written exchange strips out all the physical aspects of communication, and because of that it has a much higher potential to be misunderstood.

> ...missing the meaning of what God is communicating can lead to a whole host of problems...

In spite of the limitations of written communication, reading is still a very powerful medium of exchange. When a writer takes the time to craft the words properly, they can stimulate the senses and evoke emotions. The written word affords the reader the opportunity to slow down the exchange of information and ponder more deeply what's being said.

But because of the greater opportunity to misconstrue the meaning of written words, it's paramount that the reader strive to clearly understand the intent of the writer. This is especially true of the Bible, because missing the meaning of what God is communicating can lead to a whole host of problems, some of which can have a serious impact on our lives.

Uncovering the Author's Intent

When we read, we bring along our own personal experiences and biases, and these can have a great influence on the meaning we ascribe to the author's words. Although the Bible is a holy book that contains the words of God, thankfully we don't need a secret "decoder ring" to determine what He is saying (For those who are too young to remember, a decoder ring was a children's toy that came as a promotional device in cereal boxes and was very popular from the early 1940's up through roughly the 1970's. The decoder ring held the key to codes for writing or unlocking secret messages).

Although God's Word isn't written using special codes, we still must learn to handle the words properly in order to understand the message it's intended to convey.

Correctly Handling the Word of God

Sometimes people criticize the Bible by saying, "You can get the Bible to say anything you want it to," or, "The Bible is full of contradictions, so you can't trust it." In some ways this is true, but that's only the case when people mishandle the Bible by twisting it to say things that the Author never intended it to say.

A number of years ago someone attempted to discredit me by misquoting something I had said. Although the words they quoted were accurate, they misrepresented the meaning of my words by removing them from the context in which I said them, and by only quoting a portion of them, leaving off many key parts. In essence, they improperly "cut my words" from the conversation in such a way that they could mean something entirely different than what I had intended.

Cutting God's words out of the context in such a way that we alter His meaning is something God explicitly says we must not do. We must take care to correctly handle His Word, always seeking to discern His intended meaning.

2 Timothy 2:15 (NIV)
Do your best to present yourself to God as one approved, a worker who does not need to be ashamed and who correctly handles the word of truth.

The words "correctly handling" are translated from the Greek word "orthotomeō," which literally means to "cut straight." Just like someone quoting our words, they are only correct when the words are "cut straight" from the conversation. Anything other than a "right cutting" results in mishandling. Obviously, if we are misquoting or misapplying what the Bible says, then in actuality we no longer have God's true words. Given that the Bible contains the words of God—words that He says are more valuable than silver and gold—it is critical that we work diligently to handle, discern, and apply them properly.

> **...one very common mistake people make when reading the Bible is in failing to understand that the entire Bible isn't written specifically to them.**

Understanding Who God is Talking to

Have you ever accidentally opened a letter that wasn't addressed to you? When my mail arrives, oftentimes it consists of ten or more envelopes, and I assume that since it's in my mailbox, it's my mail. However, occasionally the mail carrier makes a mistake and one of my neighbor's envelopes ends up in my box. Over the years there have been a few times when I've opened someone else's mail because I failed to notice that it wasn't addressed to me—thankfully, it's usually just a piece of junk mail.

No matter how great the news or information is in someone else's letter, it really has no direct bearing on me. If it's an announcement that the recipient won the lottery, or a notice to appear in court, it has no effect on me because I am not the person the letter is intended for. Similarly, one very common mistake people make when reading the Bible is in failing to understand that the entire Bible isn't written specifically to them. We can certainly learn things from the entire Bible, but just like the letter intended for my neighbor, not everything in it is for me.

Jews, Gentiles, and the Followers of Christ

God loves all mankind, and part of the process of Him bringing about His plans to be reunited with man involved Him separating people into three groups: Jews, Gentiles, and the followers of Jesus. The division first began in the Old Testament when He decided to separate a particular group of Abraham's offspring (Hebrews) from the rest of the people of the world (Gentiles). Abraham's son was Isaac, and Isaac's son was Jacob. Then Jacob (also known as Israel) had twelve sons, and they became the "twelve tribes of Israel."

When we read the Old Testament, we have to realize that the majority of it was written to the Nation of Israel, the descendants of the twelve sons of Jacob. These portions of the Old Testament tell of how the people left Egypt under the leadership of Moses and formed a nation, the Law they lived by, and many pivotal events in their history. This is all great information with many things we can learn, but the things that God directed the Nation of Israel to do aren't necessarily things that we, the followers of Jesus, need to do today.

The rest of the Bible contains things that are written either for Gentiles or the followers of Christ. For instance, in the Old Testament there are prophetic pronouncements that are intended for the Gentiles, such as the nations of Edom, Moab, Egypt, etc., and in the New Testament we find many letters written as specific instructions to the followers of Jesus. These sections will oftentimes begin with phrases such as:

1 Corinthians 1:2 (NIV)
To the church of God in Corinth, to those sanctified in Christ Jesus and called to be his holy people,...

Ephesians 1:1 (NIV)
Paul, an apostle of Christ Jesus by the will of God, To God's holy people in Ephesus, the faithful in Christ Jesus...

Philippians 1:1 (NIV)
Paul and Timothy, servants of Christ Jesus, To all God's holy people in Christ Jesus at Philippi, together with the overseers and deacons...

As you can see, these sections are written to the followers of Jesus. When reading your Bible, always ask yourself, "Is God speaking here to the Jews, Gentiles, or the followers of Christ?" because a big key to enjoying the Bible involves knowing who God is speaking to.

Understanding the Language of the Bible — Literal, Figurative and Symbolic

It is also helpful to recognize that the Bible uses literal, figurative, and symbolic language. Literal language means that the words mean exactly what they say, and in general the Bible can be understood literally except where the words imply an impossibility, contradiction, or absurdity.

We use figurative phrases every day, giving it little thought because it's used to make a point or to add emphasis. If I were to say, "I was so mad that I almost exploded," you would never think that I was actually going to blow myself up with anger. Likewise, the Bible contains many figurative statements, and taking them literally can result in great misunderstandings. For instance, consider what Jesus said to a crowd: "...unless you eat the flesh of the Son of Man and drink his blood you have no life in you." If we take his words literally, we would think he was advocating cannibalism. But this was a figurative way of saying that Jesus' followers would need to be completely devoted to him.

Be aware that there are many different forms of figurative language. Working to develop an understanding of various figures of speech, irony, and so forth will increase your potential for enjoying and understanding the Bible.

The Bible is also filled with lots of symbolism, and the more we read the more we become familiar with its usage. For instance, in the Old Testament there are a number of instances where it says that someone "walked with God." This is symbolic language, and doesn't mean that someone actually walked along a path with God, but instead that they had a close relationship and fellowship with Him. Another example is how God told the Nation of Israel that He was bringing them to a land that was "flowing with milk and honey," meaning that it would be lush and very fertile. There are also numerous sections of prophecy that use symbolic language, and places where people are referred to as sheep, dogs, and cattle; Jesus is called the branch, the lion, and the morning star, and Satan is referred to as a serpent or dragon. This is all symbolic language.

Culture and Customs

As westerners, we can't help but see the Bible from the perspective of our western lives, culture, and experiences. But when we read the Bible we have to keep in mind that it's the story of an Eastern people who lived in an entirely different world with widely differing customs and cultures. There are times when the people spoken of were living a nomadic lifestyle, or were in foreign countries with other ancient cultures such as the Egyptians, Persians, or Babylonians. In addition to the Jewish culture, there are also sections of the Bible that were heavily influenced by

The reader needs to be very cautious not to impose western values on an eastern book.

Roman and other Gentile customs. The people of the Bible lived in a pre-modern time when people were more connected to nature and its cycles, such as the weather, the land, crops, and animals. It was also a time when people were very vulnerable and dependent upon one another for safety and survival, life was uncertain, and death was an ever-present reality.

These were times very unlike ours. Western society places great value on independence and self-industry, whereas the ancient cultures highly stressed social conformity, hospitality, honor, gratitude, family, and kinship. This was a world with great contrast between the rich and poor, the ruler and servant, the priest and lay-person. The reader needs to be very cautious not to impose western values on an eastern book. Learning the culture of the Bible and its different customs opens up an entirely new world to the reader.

Here are a few examples of some Biblical customs:

Greeting Another with a Kiss

Nowadays when we greet another person we usually do

so with a handshake, and if it's a close friend, possibly an embrace. In the biblical culture they would greet a friend or relative by placing their left hand on the other's right shoulder and kissing the right and then the left cheek. Knowing this helps us to understand the record of David "kissing" his best friend Jonathan (1 Samuel 20:41), and the elders in Miletus who kissed the Apostle Paul when he departed (Acts 20:37). Other records of this custom are in Genesis 27:27; 33:4; 45:15; Exodus 4:27; 18:7; and Luke 7:45.

Taking Off Your Footwear

In the East, people often removed their sandals when they entered a home because they were very dirty from the dusty roads and the filth in the streets. They also often sat on the ground with crossed legs, which would be very uncomfortable to do while wearing sandals. Taking off your footwear became a sign of respect, which is why God told Moses to remove his sandals since the ground he was standing on was considered holy (Exodus 3:5).

Washing Your Guests' Feet

Because wearing open sandals on dirty roads meant that peoples' feet would become very filthy, it was also a common practice for a servant to wash their master's feet. This courtesy was a sign of hospitality shown to a guest as a way of honoring them. Since this was most often done by a servant, Jesus' act of washing the feet of his disciples was a demonstration of great humility, an example for all of his followers to do for others (John 13:4,5). Other records of this custom are in Genesis 18:4; 19:2, 24:32; 43:24, and 1 Timothy 5:10.

These are just a few of the many customs spoken of in the Bible. Taking time to learn eastern mannerisms and customs will greatly increase our ability to understand and enjoy the Bible.

Misunderstanding and Misapplying the Bible

People frequently make the mistake of taking a section from the Bible and misapplying it to themselves. Oftentimes this happens because they either fail to recognize who God is speaking to, or they misunderstand the context in which the passage was spoken. When this happens, it is called "dislocating" the words, which can easily lead to "misapplying" them—which, in essence, is a "misuse" of God's words.

Here are a few common verses people misuse:

Philippians 4:13 (NIV)
I can do all things through him who gives me strength.

This passage is often used like a rally cry for Christians who are trying to accomplish all sorts of things. People quote this passage at sporting events, in the middle of sickness, after a flat tire, or when they run out of gas in their car. When the Apostle Paul said this, however, his message wasn't that he could really do "all things", or that God would change every negative situation for him, but that in every situation, whether famine, cold, sickness, or even in prison, he had learned to be content and to have faith in God.

Jeremiah 29:11 (NIV)
For I know the plans I have for you...plans to prosper you and not to harm you, plans to give you hope and a future.

Life is full of ups and downs, and in times of trouble people often like to quote this section as if to say, "Well, it's all part of God's plan for you." However, in the context in which this verse sits, that isn't what it's speaking about. This promise was given to the Nation of Israel, and it was about their 70-year captivity in Babylon and God's plans for their future hope and return to the Promised Land. Jeremiah told the people not to think that God had forsaken them, because He had plans to prosper them. He encouraged them to have hope because they could do well in Babylon, and then, after 70 years, their hope to have a homeland would be fulfilled and God would bring them back to their own land. This is a specific promise given to Israel, and we are misapplying it when we use it to teach that God has specific "plans to prosper" us personally today. Of course God cares for us as His children, but this is not a blanket promise for our personal prosperity the way some use it. The point is that it was His word to Israel, not directly to us today.

Genesis 31:49 (NIV)
The LORD watch between you and me when we are absent from each other.

This verse is often shared between people who move apart or live far away from each other, and they make reference to it as if it's a blessing. Unfortunately, they fail to realize that it's actually a curse. The man who was speaking it, Laban, was angry at Jacob for moving away with his daughters. He spoke this curse over the situation in the event Jacob should hurt Laban's daughters while they were separated. It may sound good to quote it, but it is another example of misapplying God's Word.

God's words are holy and powerful. He is very invested in them because what He says is what He does. They accomplish His purposes and He doesn't utter empty words or speak in vain.

Isaiah 55:10-11 (NIV)
(10) As the rain and the snow come down from heaven, and do not return to it without watering the earth and

making it bud and flourish, so that it yields seed for
the sower and bread for the eater,
(11) so is my word that goes out from my mouth: It
will not return to me empty, but will accomplish what
I desire and achieve the purpose for which I sent it.

Handling God's word properly and seeking out His
intended meaning as the Author goes a long way in helping
us learn to enjoy the Bible.

6

The Pieces of the Puzzle

Once upon a time, a father took his young son and daughter to the local parade. They lived in a small town, and as is typical with small-town parades, it included the volunteer fire department with their big, red ladder truck, an ambulance, and even some local farmers with their tractors, hay wagons, and a milk delivery truck. The parade also featured the high school band with the cheerleaders and color guard, and the local ballet school with lots of little girls dancing down the main street in their colorful dresses.

When the kids returned home, they couldn't wait to tell their mom all about the parade. The little girl was the first to speak, and the words spilled out about the beautiful girls, their colorful costumes, and all the talented dancers. But all the little boy could talk about was the firemen, their big truck, and all the farm equipment. Eventually Dad broke in and laughingly remarked, "Wow, if I didn't know any better, I would think that you kids attended two completely different parades!"

> **...whenever we focus on the parts instead of the whole, we can lose the sense of the event as a whole.**

Although the kids attended the same parade, they experienced it completely differently, as if there were two entirely different events. Why was that? Because their focus and their personal perspectives were completely different. The one parade was composed of many parts, and whenever we focus on the parts instead of the whole, we can lose the sense of the event as a whole. In other words, our perspective affects our experience.

> **The Bible is a story centered on the theme of God's rulership over His creation.**

The Fundamental Themes

Of course there is only one Bible, but our experience of it can be greatly affected by our perspective when reading it. Many people who read the Bible lose sight of the greater story that is being told and, like the kids and the parade, they end up developing a distorted view of it.

The Bible is a story centered on the theme of God's rulership over His creation. It also portrays His love for mankind, with a plot that involves a war between good and evil. As we read about the many people, places, and events, we must keep these fundamental aspects of the story in mind so that we stay on the path and don't get lost in the weeds.

The Sovereign Ruler

The Bible begins with the words, "In the beginning God created the heavens and the earth." God is the first player to set foot on the stage, and He is the central One moving behind the history of mankind. God's supremacy is the central theme of creation. He is the Creator of everything, and as such He is ruler over all. He is the King, and all His creation is His domain—also referred to as His King-dom.

Love is part of the very fabric of creation, a thread entwined through all the forces of nature.

The story of the Bible portrays how man betrayed the King, committing treason by disobeying Him. Man's act of rebellion against the King resulted in the corruption of the creation, and the Bible is the story of how God is bringing about His plan for the restoration of all creation back under His rightful rulership.

God's Love

God's love is a central element that is concurrent with the theme of His rulership. He tells us that a primary feature of His character is love; that it was because of this love that He created man; and that this love is the reason He fights for the restoration of His relationship with mankind. Love is part of the very fabric of creation, a thread entwined through all the forces of nature. It's God's love demonstrated through His faithfulness and grace that provides for all of mankind's needs.

Good and Evil

Another fundamental concept that will help us to understand the Bible is the recurrent theme of good and evil and the ever-present battle that rages between them. At various stages in His creative process, God surveyed what He did and declared it to be "very good." Thus, "good" is simply that which exists according to His intended order, and "evil" isn't some nebulous black force; it is anything existing contrary to or outside of the way God intended things to be. God set the creation up according to a certain structure, a hierarchy, and "evil" is anything which rebels against or exists contrary to that order.

Quite simply, the Bible is the story of God as the Sovereign over His creation, the Supreme Ruler who is driven by love and is working to destroy evil and restore His creation to its original state of goodness.

7

Piecing the Puzzle Together

Common Perspectives

Going back to the analogy of the jigsaw puzzle, there are two primary ways we can begin to assemble the "pieces" of the Bible. The first is to take a topical approach, and the second is to view it from a historical perspective. Below is a brief review of the topical approach of the Gospel story, and the historical approach depicting God's unfolding plan to save mankind and restore all things to proper alignment under Himself. Remember, there is only one story, one plan, and one purpose that God is moving toward, but it can be viewed from different angles.

A Topical Approach: The Simple Gospel

The word "gospel" means "good news," and one of the most important things the Bible tells is the overall story of the Good News of what God has done to restore His relationship with mankind. We should always keep the Good News in mind when reading the Bible, because it's the overall theme of God's Word.

The Gospel perspective can be broken down into five very basic parts: God, Man, Jesus, Cross, Resurrection.

- **God**

  The Bible begins with the phrase, "In the beginning, God..." Although simply stated, this is really quite profound. Included in that statement is the understanding that God, the Creator, is the only rightful ruler over all creation. God is Supreme. He is the Sovereign, the King who has the ultimate authority and power over everything.

- **Man**

  After creating the physical world, God made man and delegated to him the oversight of the earth. Unfortunately, when man disobeyed God's instructions he committed treason and transferred his dominion over the earth to God's enemy, the Devil. His act of rejecting God's command and then rebelling against Him opened the door for the tremendous physical and spiritual calamity that we see today throughout the entire creation. Disconnected from God, his true source of life, man then fell into a state of slavery to the power of sin and death.

- **Jesus**
God set in motion a plan to save mankind by promising a redeemer who would pay the price required to free mankind from sin and death. The Old Testament is the story of how God raised up a people through whom He would one day bring the promised Savior. Descriptions of the Messiah were given to prophets in the Old Testament, and Jesus conclusively demonstrated he is the "one" by fulfilling more than 300 of these prophecies.

- **Cross**
The cost of man's disobedience to God was death, and his release from sin and death could only happen if this debt of death was properly satisfied. Jesus lived in complete submission and obedience to God, which is in part what qualified him to pay the debt for all mankind by the sacrifice of his life. Jesus willingly allowed himself to die on the cross so that all who accept and follow him can be rescued from the penalty of death that has rested on mankind since the time of Adam.

- **Resurrection**
God promised that all who declare Jesus as their Lord and believe in his resurrection will, like Jesus, also be saved from everlasting death. Resurrection awaits all of mankind—some to destruction and some to everlasting life. Resurrection to everlasting life is the

ultimate Good News, and it's God's final
objective for all who love Him.

The Historical Perspective

Taking a historical view helps us to understand the various
players in the Old Testament and how God worked with them
and through various events to progress His plans. History
shows us the larger picture, which in turn helps us to make
sense of the various parts. Looking solely at the parts while not
keeping in mind the larger picture will only cause confusion.

Here is a brief synopsis of the major historical events
portrayed in the Bible:

1. The Fall of Man

The story of Adam and Eve, their disobedience toward God
and the introduction of sin, death and decay into the world.
God makes a promise that one day He will send a Savior who
will redeem man from the curse he has been placed under.

2. Call of Abraham

God chooses Abraham, a man who completely trusts and
believes in God, and He promises to make a nation from
Abraham through which "all the nations of the earth would be
blessed." (Genesis 12:1-3). This is a very important passage in
the Bible concerning salvation because it reveals God's heart
to restore all of mankind to a state of blessing. Throughout
the Bible, we see God working to bring this promise to pass.

3. Birth of Isaac

Although Abraham's wife Sarah is barren and too old to
naturally have a child, she miraculously conceives and gives

birth to their son, Isaac. This is God's way of confirming to Abraham the ultimate fulfillment of His promise that Abraham's offspring will become a great nation—even though it will come to pass a long time after Abraham is gone.

4. Twelve Sons

Isaac's son Jacob, whose name is eventually changed to Israel, has twelve sons who in time become the twelve tribes of Israel. One son, Joseph, is sold by his brothers into slavery in Egypt. Through a series of events orchestrated by God from behind the scenes, Joseph eventually becomes vice-regent to Pharaoh. During a famine, Israel's family comes to Egypt where Joseph cares for them. When the famine is over, they decide to stay in Egypt, where they multiply greatly and are eventually enslaved by the Egyptians.

5. The Exodus

The Israelites cry out to God and He raises up Moses, a prophet, who delivers them from Egypt. Pharaoh does not want to let Israel go, but relents after several devastating plagues upon Egypt. Through a series of supernatural events done by God's hand, the power of Egypt is completely broken as Pharaoh and his army perish in the sea while pursuing the Israelites in an attempt to recapture them. The news of these events and the miraculous movements of God with Israel spreads throughout the surrounding nations.

6. The Law

During their wilderness wanderings, God fashions the descendants of Israel into a nation by giving them a system of ordinances and instructions called the Law in order to govern them as a select people by regulating their sacrifices, moral behavior, and social customs. The Law is central to the identity of Israel and separates them from all the other people on the earth. The Law provides special blessings to the people when they obey, as well as curses when they don't.

7. Conquering the Land

Part of the promise God made to Abraham involved his offspring inheriting a particular area of land that is known today as Israel. It is also called the "Promised Land," because God promised it to Abraham and his descendants. After wandering in the desert for 40 years, the Israelites finally enter this land and conquer it under the initial leadership of Joshua, Moses' successor as the leader of Israel. Then begins a period of more than 350 years where the people go through seven cycles of rebellion and disobedience resulting in a downward spiral into moral and spiritual chaos. The pattern is:

- Sin—the people disobey, commit idolatry, and forget the Lord God.
- Oppression—an oppressor comes and conquers Israel.
- Prayer—the people cry out to God for help.
- Deliverance—God hears their cry and sends a deliverer to rescue them.
- Rest—the people and the land enjoy rest and prosperity until the cycle begins again.

8. The United Kingdom and Three Kings: Saul, David & Solomon

Tiring of the cycle of oppressions and deliverance, the people want to be led by a king who will physically sit on a throne, just like in the other nations of the world—rather than having God as their king. Saul is chosen, a man who fits all the physical characteristics of what the people expect a king to be. Unfortunately, Saul's deep character flaws of fearfulness and people-pleasing become his downfall.

Next, David is selected by God to succeed Saul as king, not because David is perfect but because he has incredible devotion and passion for God—he is a "man after God's own heart." Ultimately, God makes a promise to David that his kingdom will never end, an indication that the Messiah will be one of David's descendants.

Following David's death, his son Solomon ascends to the throne and, although he is considered to be the wisest man on the earth, his idolatry and disobedience to God sets the stage for great calamity which results in the splitting of the kingdom.

9. The Kingdom Splits (Israel and Judah)

Following the sin of Solomon, the united kingdom of Israel splits into two kingdoms. The northern kingdom, consisting of ten tribes, retains the name "Israel." The southern kingdom is called "Judah," and it consists of two tribes—Judah and Benjamin. This begins a time of great rivalry between the two kingdoms.

10. The Assyrian Dispersion

After 200 years and 19 kings, in 722 BC the northern kingdom falls to an invading army of the Assyrians, a pagan nation in the north. The people of Israel are dispersed by the Assyrians throughout their empire and foreigners are brought in to occupy their lands. These foreigners become known as the Samaritans and are despised by the true Israelites. The ten northern tribes remain dispersed and have never returned to the land. Part of the prophecy of the future is that God will eventually bring Israel back home.

11. The Babylonian Captivity

The southern kingdom of Judah survives for approximately 350 years, from the time of the split of the united kingdom in 922 BC until the temple is burned and their kings replaced in 586 BC. There are a total of 20 southern kings, and while some are righteous, most aren't. Judah eventually declines to the point where God's patience with them runs out. The Judeans are taken into captivity in Babylon in waves, beginning in 605 BC when Nebuchadnezzar invades Judah and takes captives back with him (Jeremiah 15:1., Daniel 1:1). The Babylonian captivity of Judah lasts 70 years, and then the Persians, who conquer Babylon, let them return to the Promised Land.

12. Returning to the Land

God's promises for His people are tied to their presence in the Promised Land of Canaan, and likewise God's displeasure, discipline, and judgment against them result in their expulsion from it for 70 years. At the end of 70 years, after they repent, God allows the Judeans to return to the land of Israel. However, the Judeans' repeated failure to honor the Law results in God declaring that the time will come when he will abolish the covenant of the Law and will make a new covenant—a time when the Law will be written on the hearts of mankind. This is a promise pointing to the coming of Christ and his rulership in the Millennial Kingdom (Jeremiah 31:35-37).

13. The Messiah Comes

The Israelites continue to live with the expectation that God will one day deliver them by sending a king, a political rescuer who will save them from the tyranny they endure under the Romans. Like David, he will be a military hero known as the Son of David, and he will free them from political oppression, ushering in a time of restoration and freedom.

What they fail to understand is that the king will come two times. First, he will come as the "suffering servant" who will be afflicted with the penalty of mankind's sins; then he will come a second time as the conquering King. Because of this mistake in their understanding, many Jews fail to recognize that Jesus is the Messiah when he comes for the first time.

The four Gospels—Matthew, Mark, Luke, and John—tell of the story of Jesus' first coming—his birth, life, death, and resurrection. They conclude with his instructions for mankind and the promise of his return, when he will reign as the King of Kings over his Millennial Kingdom.

14. The Coming of Holy Spirit

Upon his departure, Jesus instructs his followers to wait in Jerusalem, where he will send them "power from on high," the promised holy spirit. From the day on which the gift of holy spirit is poured out, all who accept Jesus as their Lord and believe that God has raised him from the dead freely receive the same holy spirit, a token and guarantee of everlasting life. Those who accept Jesus are called "Christians" and "the Sons of God," and we await the return of Jesus when we will reign with him in his kingdom on earth.

15. Christ Returns

As Jesus predicted, the day is coming when he will return to earth. Although there are a lot of different events involved, in summary, Jesus will return to earth, conquer it, and rid it of evildoers; he will then set up his kingdom on earth as a paradise, fulfilling the prophecy that "the meek will inherit the earth." (Matthew 5:5)

16. The Final End

Even though the earth under Jesus' rule will be a paradise, amazingly, some people will become discontented and rebel against him. There will be a final war followed by a judgment, and then the New Jerusalem, with streets of gold, will come down from heaven to earth. In the end, Jesus will deliver everything over to God, the Creator and Righteous Ruler of the Universe.

> **The individual pieces of the Bible aren't nearly as important as the whole.**

The historical view helps us to keep track of God's actions over time with the major players and events. As we read the Bible, we must remember that its purpose isn't for people to take individual parts and remove them from their context in the overall story. The individual pieces of the Bible aren't nearly as important as the whole. Just like with language, it's the sentence that gives meaning to the words, and the paragraph that helps us understand the meaning of the individual sentences. The picture of God's rulership, His love, and the battle between good and evil is what brings meaning to the individual stories in the Bible.

8

Covenants and Dispensations

Growing up, I was fascinated with science, especially with the way the human body worked. Part of my fascination came from an illustrated book we owned, titled "The Human Body." It was filled with hundreds of detailed pictures and diagrams of the various parts of the body and its systems.

One of the most interesting features of the book was a section in the middle with a number of clear pages, each depicting a different aspect of the body. It began with an overview of a man, and as every page was turned, a different layer was removed from his body. With the first page went the skin, revealing the muscles, ligaments, and blood vessels, followed by the nerves, organs, and so forth on subsequent pages, until all that remained was the skeletal structure.

Although that science book was a great aid to understanding the various systems in the human body, the reality is that none of those systems can operate independently from each other. They are all interwoven parts of the whole. It's great to study the muscles, but one must bear in mind that they are only viable because of the nerves that excite them, the blood vessels that feed them, and the bones that they are attached to.

Like the human body, in learning to enjoy the Bible we must take care that we don't become so focused on the particular parts that we lose sight of the whole. It's not a book of independent sayings. Taking a systematic approach to the topics in the Bible can greatly aid our learning, but we must always bear in mind that the parts function only in the context of the bigger picture.

Understanding Covenants

In addition to a topical or historical approach, it's also very helpful for us to understand that covenants are an important part of the Bible. A covenant is a legally binding agreement, and those found in the Bible are a big key to understanding God's actions throughout history. By understanding the various covenants in the Bible we can see how, since the time of Adam, God has progressively revealed aspects of His plans and purposes.

> A covenant in the Bible is much more than a promise; it's a sacred agreement between God and man...

A covenant in the Bible is much more than a promise; it's a sacred agreement between God and man, each one a milestone marker in the road of history indicating what God is doing to save mankind. Below is a brief summary of the major covenants that God made:

The Covenant in Eden

In the Garden of Eden, there was a promise of stewardship and dominion between God and Adam. In return for Adam's proper care of the earth and the animals, God gave him rulership over them. Adam was to be fruitful and multiply, and he was also to "work [the Garden] and take care of it." (Genesis 2:15 NIV) Man was obligated to obey God, specifically to not eat from the tree of the knowledge of good and evil, and if he disobeyed then the penalty would be death.

Genesis 1:28 (NIV)

God blessed them and said to them, "Be fruitful and increase in number; fill the earth and subdue it. Rule over the fish in the sea and the birds in the sky and over every living creature that moves on the ground."

Genesis 2:15-17 (NIV)

(15) The LORD God took the man and put him in the Garden of Eden to work it and take care of it.
(16) And the LORD God commanded the man, "You are free to eat from any tree in the garden;
(17) but you must not eat from the tree of the knowledge of good and evil, for when you eat from it you will certainly die."

Hosea 6:7 (NIV)

As at Adam, they have broken the covenant; they were unfaithful to me there.

The Covenant with Adam

Adam violated his promise to God, which God had told him beforehand was punishable by death. However, instead of Adam dying immediately, God's grace and mercy allowed for an animal to be substituted temporarily for him. God further promised that He would one day send a redeemer who would rescue mankind from sin and death. This was the very first revealing by God to man that His plan involved a redeemer who would suffer but who would also crush the head of God's enemy, the Devil.

Genesis 3:15 (NIV)

And I will put enmity between you and the woman, and between your offspring and hers; he will crush your head, and you will strike his heel."

The Covenant with Noah

In response to mankind's great evil and wickedness, God executed judgment and flooded the earth, killing everyone except for Noah and his immediate family. In response to Noah's obedience and his honoring of God, God promised that He would never again destroy life on earth with a flood. The rainbow was established as a sign of God's promise.

Genesis 9:11-13 (NIV)

(11) I establish my covenant with you: Never again will all life be destroyed by the waters of a flood...

(12) And God said, "This is the sign of the covenant I am making between me and you and every living creature with you, a covenant for all generations to come:

(13) I have set my rainbow in the clouds, and it will be the sign of the covenant between me and the earth.

The Covenant with Abraham

Following the Flood of Noah, people began to multiply once again and replenish the earth. About 400 years later, God called Abraham (originally known as Abram), directing him to leave the land of his fathers and travel west to an area now known as Israel—the Promised Land. In response to Abraham's trust in God, God promised him that he would have numerous offspring and would be the father of many nations. (Genesis 17:4) God also promised that through Abraham's offspring all the nations of the world would be blessed (Genesis 12:3), a clear reference to the Messiah coming from Abraham's descendants.

Genesis 22:17-18 (NIV)

(17) I will surely bless you and make your descendants as numerous as the stars in the sky and as the sand on the seashore. Your descendants will take possession of the cities of their enemies,

(18) and through your offspring all nations on earth will be blessed, because you have obeyed me."

This covenant further revealed God's plan of redemption, and He reiterated it to Abraham's descendants, specifically Isaac, Jacob, and the Nation of Israel.

The Covenant through Moses

The twelve sons of Jacob (whose name was changed to Israel) and all of their families traveled to Egypt during a famine. Their offspring stayed there and were eventually enslaved by the Egyptians. Faithful to His promise, many years later God worked through Moses to bring them out of Egypt and to the land He had promised to Abraham.

God established a covenant with the Nation of Israel that He would provide for and protect them as long as they faithfully obeyed and served Him. This is oftentimes referred to as the Mosaic covenant, because God delivered it to Moses as the mediator between Himself and Israel. It included stipulations concerning their religious practices, moral behavior, governance, and culture, such as diet, clothing, cleansing, etc.

Most people are familiar with aspects of this covenant, such as the Ten Commandments; the covenant became commonly known as the Law. There were a few purposes for the Law, such as to separate the Nation of Israel as a distinct people from the rest of the world through whom God was going to bring the Messiah. It also demonstrated what having a holy relationship with God required, and most importantly, it pointed to the need for a redeemer.

The Covenant with David

David was the second king of Israel, and although he committed a number of serious sins, he humbly repented of his misdeeds and sought to serve God with great passion. God even said that David "was a man after God's own heart," and in response to David's faithfulness, He promised that there would never be an end to his kingdom—an indication to David that the Messiah, the King of Kings, would be a descendant of his.

> **2 Samuel 7:8; 16 (NIV)**
> (8) Now then, tell my servant David, 'This is what the LORD Almighty says: I took you from the pasture, from tending the flock, and appointed you ruler over my people Israel…
> (16) Your house and your kingdom will endure forever before me; your throne will be established forever.

The New Covenant

After hundreds and hundreds of years of the people of Israel repeatedly failing to fulfill their side of the Mosaic covenant, God indicated that He would abolish the Covenant of the Law and institute a New Covenant, the Covenant of Grace. God revealed through the Prophet Jeremiah that a time would come when everyone would know the Lord; His law would be in their minds and written upon their hearts, and all of their sins would be forgiven.

Jeremiah 31:31-34 (NIV)

(31) "The days are coming," declares the LORD, "when I will make a new covenant with the people of Israel and with the people of Judah.

(32) It will not be like the covenant I made with their ancestors when I took them by the hand to lead them out of Egypt, because they broke my covenant, though I was a husband to them, " declares the LORD.

(33) "This is the covenant I will make with the people of Israel after that time," declares the LORD. "I will put my law in their minds and write it on their hearts. I will be their God, and they will be my people.

(34) No longer will they teach their neighbor, or say to one another, 'Know the LORD,' because they will all know me, from the least of them to the greatest," declares the LORD. "For I will forgive their wickedness and will remember their sins no more."

This was the new covenant that Jesus established through his sacrificial death, but the fullness of it won't be realized until he comes in the future and establishes his Millennial Kingdom on earth.

Understanding the various covenants provides us with significant information about what God is doing as He executes His plan of redemption.

Understanding Administrations in the Bible

In the United States, we elect a President who serves as the head of the executive branch of government. In the 200-plus years since the founding of our nation, we have had over forty Presidents, and when we view their performances we can see that there are clear differences in the way each has governed. We call these terms their "administrations," meaning their "way of governing." Similarly, there are differing "Administrations" (also known as "dispensations") in the Bible—different ways that God has governed and dealt with man over time.

...we can see that there are clear and distinct periods throughout history where God has governed differently.

When we view the Bible through a dispensational lens, we can see that there are clear and distinct periods throughout history where God has governed differently. Going back to the analogy of the book on the human body, dispensationalism is another type of clear acetate laid over the history of mankind.

Below are 8 ways some dispensationalists observe the spiritual history of man and the movements of God:

The Age of Innocence (or "Original Paradise")

This was the time in the Garden of Eden when man lacked knowledge of good and evil. This dispensation ended when man sinned and was expelled from the Garden, and mankind, the animals, and the earth fell under a curse.

The Age of Conscience

After being forced out of the Garden, man was still required to live rightly before God, which meant that he had to resist his desire to sin. God allowed people to offer a substitutionary sacrifice—a temporary covering for their sin.

People were still answerable to God for their actions and it was up to them to govern according to their conscience.

Unfortunately, all of mankind became extremely wicked over time, so in His righteous judgment God sent a flood and wiped out all mankind except for Noah and his family. God promised to never flood the earth in judgment again, and this dispensation closed after the Flood.

The Age of Civil Government

Following the Flood of Noah, God established a covenant that he would no longer execute His justice and judgment upon humanity through a flood. He also instructed Noah to multiply and replenish the earth. It was during this time that man was responsible for governing his own affairs and that he had the authority and responsibility to enact the death penalty (Genesis 6:9). Man continued to rebel against God by building the tower of Babel, and God responded by confusing languages, which caused the people to disperse throughout the world. God then called Abraham, made a covenant with him, and ultimately raised up Abraham's descendants through Isaac and Jacob as the Nation of Israel.

The Age of The Law

God heard the cry of the Israelites in Egypt and worked through Moses as His agent to bring them out of captivity. After the Exodus, God entered into a new covenant with the Nation of Israel: the Covenant of the Law. The Law served the following purposes:

1. It established Israel as a nation.
2. It provided a governmental structure (a combination of the sacred and the secular).
3. It created religious distance between Israel and the pagan nations.

4. It provided restraint for the evils of society.
5. It offered instruction in fruitful living and how best to live life.
6. It clearly defined sin and unholy behavior.
7. It served as a tutor and instructor until Christ.
8. It stood as a means of salvation (through faith).

Sadly, Israel repeatedly disobeyed God and underwent several cycles of punishment during the leadership of various judges and kings; they were eventually dispersed or enslaved after the period of kings.

Then the Messiah (Jesus) came; he was faithful to fulfill the whole Law, and established the New Covenant foretold by Jeremiah. The New Covenant was instituted with the death of Christ, and about 40 years later the final vestiges of the Mosaic Law were removed with the destruction of the Temple.

The Age of Grace

After Jesus inaugurated the New Covenant, the gift of holy spirit was given on the Day of Pentecost, and it's still given to this day to all who accept Christ as their Lord and believe God has raised him from the dead (Romans 10:9-10). This is only a token of the fullness of the spirit that will be given when all of the New Covenant promises are realized as Jesus rules his Millennial Kingdom on earth.

The Administration of Grace is the age in which we now live, and one of the differences from past administrations that we enjoy is that those who become children of God by spiritual birth receive the gift of holy spirit and are no longer either Jews or Gentiles. Collectively, we are all referred to as members of the Body of Christ. He is our head and he is directing us as members of his Body. Many believe this age will come to an end when Jesus gathers the members of his

Body in an event commonly known as "the Rapture," a time when, in an instant, those who died having believed in Christ, and the living believers, will be given new bodies and taken up with Jesus to be with him forever.

The Age of Wrath

Following the Age of Grace, there will be a period of time, commonly believed to last for 7 years, in which the Devil will attempt to rule the entire world under one leader, a man devoted to him. This man will be called the "Son of Perdition" (KJV) or the Antichrist. This will be a time of great persecution and suffering, and, at some point during it, God will pour out His judgment, also known as His Wrath, upon mankind. This age will come to an end when Jesus returns with the armies of heaven, fights the Battle of Armageddon, conquers the earth, and binds Satan and casts him into prison for 1,000 years.

The Millennial Kingdom

During this age, Jesus will physically rule the earth for 1,000 years, and it will be completely healed and be a "paradise." There are many Old Testament prophecies which indicate this will be a wonderful time of peace and safety, without sickness or war, and God will fulfill many of the promises He made to Abraham and his descendants concerning the Promised Land.

This Age will close with a final battle between the forces of good and evil. Satan and his followers will then be judged and destroyed in the Lake of Fire.

The Eternal Kingdom

In the Eternal Kingdom, the faithful will live forever with God and the Lord Jesus in the New Jerusalem, a heavenly city prepared by God for all who are faithful and love Him. Very few details are actually revealed about this final age.

By understanding the Covenants and various administrational changes in the Bible, we can gain a much greater understanding of how to put the pieces of the puzzle together. Although there are many ways we can view the story that is told in the Bible, what remains is that there is only one theme throughout: the theme of God's rightful rulership.

1 Corinthians 15:24-28 (NIV)
(24) Then the end will come, when [Jesus] hands over the kingdom to God the Father after he has destroyed all dominion, authority and power.
(25) For he must reign until he has put all his enemies under his feet.
(26) The last enemy to be destroyed is death.
(27) For he "has put everything under his feet." Now when it says that "everything" has been put under him, it is clear that this does not include God himself, who put everything under Christ.
(28) When he has done this, then the Son himself will be made subject to him who put everything under him, so that God may be all in all.

Once Jesus has brought everything back into the proper order—the order that God set in place "in the beginning"— then he will deliver it back to God, at which time God will once again say, "It is all very good."

9

Enjoying the Bible

The Bible is like a tapestry woven of many threads that collectively come together to make a beautiful work. It's not simply a book that is intended to tell a story; it conveys to mankind the very heart of God, His desires, and the story of His plans and purposes.

The first step in learning to enjoy the Bible begins when we simply start reading it. Remember that although the Bible tells a story, it doesn't do so the way a novel does. The story of the Bible is revealed through the timeline of history that it records. As we see how God has interacted with mankind, we see the unfolding of His plans and purposes.

Reading for Encouragement and Inspiration

There are times when we should simply read the Bible for the pure enjoyment of it, for inspiration and encouragement. As we read about how God has cared for others, we can be encouraged in knowing that He loves and always cares for us, too. It's comforting to see that many of the characters in the Bible struggled with some of the same flaws we all have, especially when we see that in spite of those flaws God always loved them and forgave them when they repented.

Reading to Gain Insight and Wisdom

The Bible is a source of timeless wisdom, insights into life that are ageless and passed down to us from antiquity. It is a great resource for wisdom with its many clever sayings and examples. These are words that, if we learn and follow them, will help us to get the most out of life; wisdom that will help us to establish proper relationships with others, set the right priorities in life, handle our finances and possessions correctly, and learn how to follow the right, fair, and just path of life.

Reading for Learning

Reading the Bible with the general intent of learning can also be a very enriching experience. When we approach the Bible in this manner, we begin to see the advancement of mankind from its historical beginnings. We may also find it very helpful to take notes so that we can then look to sources outside of the Bible that will help to explain biblical customs and historical records; an atlas can also help us to become familiar with the locations and geography in Scripture. Reading for learning can expand our personal view of the world if we approach it with an attitude toward developing an understanding about different times, peoples, and cultures.

Reading for Spiritual Insight

It has been rightly said that God has a purpose for everything He says, where He says it, to whom He says it, and how He says it. We must never forget that the Bible is the Word of God, and as such, it's a spiritual book which conveys spiritual insights about the true nature of life, the interaction between the physical and spiritual realms, the spiritual battle, and the nature of the forces of good and evil. Reading the Bible helps us to understand what it means for God to be the Creator, a holy God, and a loving Father.

> **What's important is to not get overwhelmed in the details, but instead to pursue God with all your heart.**

Through the course of this book I have sought to give you some background on the Bible and a cursory overview of the picture it portrays, so that you can have a framework in which to fit the puzzle pieces together. There is no need to be intimidated by the Bible; know that God greatly desires for you to know and love Him the way He knows and loves you. What's important is to not get overwhelmed in the details, but instead to pursue God with all your heart. Learning to enjoy the Bible will be one of your greatest steps toward growing closer to God and experiencing His faithful love and goodness. It's time to start learning to enjoy the Bible!

A Quick Reference to the
Books of the Bible

The following is a very brief synopsis of each of the books of the Bible, and it's intended to give the novice reader a sense of each Book and how it fits with in the overall picture of the Bible. It's highly recommended that the reader refer to additional reference sources for a more complete explanation and understanding of each of the Books of the Bible.

- The Old Testament -

The Old Testament is the first major section of the Christian Bible, and it's composed of 39 individual books. The first five books, written by Moses, tell of the rise of mankind, the call of Abraham, and the formation of the Nation of Israel. The other books pertain to wisdom and poetry, the history of Israel, the Law of Moses, and various prophets. It's called the "Old Testament," meaning the "Old Covenant," as a reference to the covenant God made with Israel when He instituted the Law through Moses.

- The Torah -

The first five books of the Bible are called the Torah—a Hebrew word meaning "instruction." They are also referred to as the Pentateuch, meaning "five scrolls."

Genesis

The Book of Genesis is the book of beginnings. It focuses on God's creative actions, the Fall of Adam and Eve, the degradation of the human race and the corruption of the world. Following the Flood of Noah, God calls Abraham, a man who completely trusts God and to whom God makes a promise that he will be the father of many nations and through his offspring all the people of the world will be blessed. This is a promise that the Redeemer will come one day through Abraham's bloodline.

Exodus

Exodus means "the departure," and this book portrays the departure of Israel from Egypt after years of captivity. During their 40 years of travel in the wilderness, they receive the Law of Moses, a covenant that God makes with them in which He promises to provide for them as long as they are faithful in their obedience to Him.

Leviticus

One of the twelve tribes of Israel was the Levites, and the book of Leviticus focuses on the duties and responsibilities of the Levites in leading the Nation of Israel in their worship of God, as well as on laws and regulations to keep Israel holy before God.

Numbers

The book of Numbers tells of the 40-year wanderings of Israel in the wilderness of Sinai. It begins with Moses and Aaron taking a census, includes a description of the people's failure to trust God when they come to the Promised Land, and describes their punishment: that the older generation must all die before the younger can enter the land.

Deuteronomy

Deuteronomy literally means "second law", and it's the book that records Moses' repetition of the Law, as well as adding some additional laws that are necessary for life in the Promised Land. Moses encourages the people's faithfulness to God and exhorts them to be obedient as they enter the Promised Land.

- Historical Books -

Following the first five books of Moses, there are 12 books containing the historical accounts of the Nation of Israel during the time of the united kingdom, the splitting of Judah and Israel, and their dispersion under the Assyrians and carrying away into Babylonian captivity.

Joshua

When Moses dies, the mantle of leadership is passed on to his assistant, Joshua. Joshua leads Israel into the Promised Land and wages numerous military campaigns in conquest of the land. After conquering most of the land under Joshua's leadership, the land is divided among the twelve tribes.

Judges

Following the death of Joshua, the Israelites undergo a period of about 350 years involving a repeating cycle of sin, oppression, repentance, deliverance, and rest. The Book of Judges includes some remarkable stories of the people who judge Israel, such as Ehud, Deborah, Gideon, and Samson.

Ruth

This is a beautiful story that takes place during the same period as the book of Judges. Ruth, a Moabitess, marries a young Israelite who dies. Instead of returning to her family, Ruth stays with her mother-in-law, demonstrating great love, faithfulness, and devotion to her. Eventually Ruth remarries and becomes the great-grandmother of King David, through whom the Messiah comes. Ruth is a story of grace and mercy, demonstrating the principle of the "kinsman redeemer"—that is, a near relative who redeems someone from difficult circumstances—as a foreshadowing of the Messiah.

1 & 2 Samuel

Samuel is the last judge before Israel demands a king like all of the other nations around them. Samuel anoints Saul, the first king, and also the young boy David when Saul fails to obey God. 2 Samuel provides an account of the reign of David the warrior king, his missteps, and his wonderful heart to serve God.

1 & 2 Kings

Starting with King Solomon, the books of 1 & 2 Kings tell the stories of the various kings who rule the divided kingdoms of Israel in the north and Judah in the south. Eventually, the kingdoms fall because of disobedience to God and are judged for their idolatry.

1 & 2 Chronicles

These books cover the same general timeframes as 1 & 2 Kings. They cover much of the same material, but with different details. Many consider them to be written with a spiritual context.

Ezra

Ezra tracks the restoration of the people to the land of Israel following their captivity in Babylon. Under Ezra's leadership, the people begin rebuilding the Temple.

Nehemiah

Nehemiah is a contemporary of Ezra and it's under his leadership that, against great opposition, the walls of Jerusalem are rebuilt. Ezra and Nehemiah are the last books of the Old Testament chronologically.

Esther

Prior to the Israelites' return to Jerusalem under the leadership of Ezra, the Persians conquer Babylon. During the reign of the Persians there is a plot to exterminate all of the Jews, but God raises up Esther to become queen and through her He saves His people.

- Books of Wisdom and Poetry -

One can easily recognize the differences in the style of literature when comparing the books of law and history to the books of wisdom and poetry.

Job

Some scholars believe that this is the oldest book in the Bible. It opens with a scene of the spiritual dynamics taking place between God and His nemesis, the Devil. It portrays the suffering of Job and demonstrates how even the righteous suffer now, that our suffering isn't necessarily the result of our personal sin, and that in all situations we must stay faithful to God because He is always faithful to us.

Psalms

This is the longest book in the Bible with 150 individual psalms. It's a collection of Hebrew poetry and song lyrics, many of them written by King David. Most are praises and prayers to God, dealing with the subjects of creation, worship, sin, justice, righteousness, and God's protection.

Proverbs

This book is known as the "book of wisdom," and its primary purpose is to teach the young and inexperienced how best to live life. Many of the proverbs are credited to Solomon, King David's son, the wisest man who has ever lived. Proverbs says that it will give the reader wisdom so that they will know the right, fair, and just path of life.

Ecclesiastes

Like the book of Proverbs, this book was also written by King Solomon, and it contains many maxims and wise sayings. It was written to show future generations the pain and depression that comes from the meaningless pursuit of money, power, sensual pleasure, and other earthly endeavors. The book concludes by pointing out that everyone will inevitably die, so without God and our obedience to Him, all man's endeavors are meaningless.

Song of Solomon

This is a book of prose written about the love between a man and a woman. It points out the joys of love and even of sex, and foreshadows the great love that Jesus will have for his "bride," the body of believers.

- Prophetic Books -

Throughout the span of history, God has spoken to His people through His prophets. He established various covenants (Abraham, Moses, and David) and called people back to them through the prophets. It wasn't the role of the prophets to manage the day-to-day affairs of the people, but to provide them with guidance and special revelation that pertained to God's plans and purposes.

- Major Prophets -

Isaiah

This book tells the story of a prophet from the tribe of Judah whom God raises up to warn of the coming Assyrian dispersion and Babylonian captivity. Isaiah also predicts the coming of the Persian king Cyrus who will release Judah and allow them to return to the Land. In addition to his message of judgment, Isaiah also delivers many comforting prophecies concerning the coming Messiah and his kingdom.

Jeremiah

Known as the "weeping Prophet," Jeremiah speaks of the coming dark days of Judah's deportation to Babylon. The record of Jeremiah shows how, as a result of speaking truthfully for God, he suffers greatly at the hands of wicked rulers. Suffering for speaking the truth is one of the themes of the Bible, and in that suffering Jeremiah certainly foreshadows the suffering of Jesus Christ. Eventually, Jeremiah's words come to pass and Israel is conquered and carried off to Babylon.

Lamentations

Although technically a book of poetry, Lamentations contains Jeremiah's mourning following the fall of Jerusalem.

The walls of the city have been torn down, the glory of Jerusalem is gone, and all that the people can do now is mourn and hope. Lamentations shows us that there is no sin in mourning when disaster occurs, but that we should always combine it with hope.

Ezekiel

Jerusalem is conquered in a series of three waves. During this time, God raises up a contemporary of Jeremiah, a young priest named Ezekiel, who serves as a "watchman on the wall"—warning the people but also encouraging them with the vision of the new Temple of the Lord in the Millennial Kingdom.

Daniel

Carried off into captivity as a young boy, Daniel is raised to serve in kings' courts with the schooling of wise advisors. He survives the Persian conquest of Babylon and rises to a prominent position of power in the Persian Empire. Daniel shows us that even if our circumstances are undesirable, God is with us and we can prosper. Daniel is also given remarkable visions concerning the end times.

- Minor Prophets -

The following books are considered the "minor prophets," not because they are of little importance, but because their books are shorter, limited in scope, and more narrow in focus. The major and minor prophets tend to be the least-read books in the Bible, primarily because they can be difficult to understand given that they usually contain condemnations of the sinful behavior of various peoples and kings.

Hosea

Hosea prophesies to Israel, the unfaithful northern

kingdom. This book contains a record of how God uses Hosea and his marriage as a symbol of Israel's unfaithfulness.

Joel

The book of Joel is only three chapters long. It's a call for Judah, the southern kingdom, to repent and return to God. Joel also prophesies about the end times.

Amos

Amos is a contemporary of Hosea and Isaiah. He is a shepherd and a farmer, and even though he lacks a priestly background, God calls him and sends him to the northern kingdom of Israel because of their corruption, neglect of God's word, idolatry, greed, and oppression of the poor.

Obadiah

With only 21 verses, this is the shortest book in the Old Testament. Obadiah condemns the Gentile kingdom of Edom for their sins against God and Israel.

Jonah

God calls a man named Jonah to warn Nineveh, a city in the nation of Assyria, of God's coming judgment unless they repent. Instead, Jonah tries to run from his mission from God. His disobedience results in personal calamity; he is thrown overboard from the ship he was using to escape from God, where he is swallowed by a large fish, dies, and is in the fish for 3 days and nights—a foreshadowing of Jesus' time in the grave before his resurrection. Jonah is then brought back to life, repents, and finally does what God asked him to do—in spite of some additional complaints.

Micah

Micah condemns the leadership of Israel—its rulers, priests and prophets—for their exploitation of the people. The book is a warning of judgment, but it also includes a message of hope and restoration as well as a prophecy that the Messiah will be born in Bethlehem (Micah 5:2).

Nahum

This is a book written after the fall of Israel to the Assyrians, and in it Nahum foretells that Nineveh, capital of Assyria, will suffer severe consequences for their sin and brutal treatment of Israel.

Habakkuk

The prophet Habakkuk questions God, asking Him why He is allowing His people to suffer. God replies, and the prophet's faith is restored.

Zephaniah

The prophet Zephaniah writes before the fall of Judah as a warning of coming judgment and a call for repentance. He also foretells a day when a remnant of the people will return from exile.

Haggai

Haggai challenges God's people concerning their priorities after they return from captivity in Babylon. They have done little to restore God's Temple and have instead focused on their own projects and homes. The prophet promises restoration and blessings from God if the people will do what is right and put God's Temple first.

Zechariah

This book includes a call for God's people to do what is right, to administer justice, and to never oppress the needy. He also prophesies concerning the Messiah and the end times.

Malachi

Malachi calls out to God's people who have forsaken His commands. He reproves the priests who are sacrificing blemished animals and not taking their roles seriously. Malachi predicts the coming of John the Baptist (Malachi 3:1-6). The close of Malachi begins a period of about 400 years of silence during which no prophets add to the Scriptures.

- New Testament -

The New Testament is the second major section of the Christian Bible, and it's composed of 27 separate books. The New Testament chronicles the life and teachings of Jesus in four Gospels, then traces the actions of his first followers and the spread of Jesus' teachings in the first century through the Book of Acts and 21 letters written between Jesus' followers, and concludes with the Book of Revelation, a book of prophecy that focuses on end time events. This section is called the "New Testament", meaning the "New Covenant" between God and mankind that Jesus established, as prophesied in the book of Jeremiah.

Gospels

Each of the four Gospels is a narrative of the life, death, and resurrection of Jesus. They include many of Jesus' teachings and speak of him from differing perspectives, collectively forming a fourfold portrait of Christ.

Matthew

This book presents a portrait of Jesus as a king from the line of David. The phrase "the kingdom of heaven," a reference to the time when Jesus will reign on earth as the King of Kings, occurs more than 30 times in Matthew. The phrase "Son of David" is also used ten times, another reference to his kingship.

Mark

In Mark, Jesus is depicted as a humble servant. Emphasis is placed on his "doing," and the language is simple and forceful, underscoring the works he did as a servant instead of his words (teaching).

Luke

This Gospel places greater focus on the humanity of Jesus, opening with his birth and presentation at the Temple and showing that he was subject to his parents like all children are. He is also depicted as a warm, loving, kind, and compassionate person. Additionally, in this book we see his great concern for the poor and less fortunate.

John

The Gospel of John emphasizes Jesus as the only begotten Son of God. Jesus refers to God as a "Father" more times in this book than in all of the other Gospels combined. The writer makes it clearly known at the end of this Gospel that its purpose is to help people believe in Jesus as the Messiah, the Son of God.

- History -

Acts

This book is a narrative of the history of the first-century followers of Christ, and it includes a description of their activities right after Jesus' death as it follows the spread of Christianity.

- Letters of Paul -

The Apostle Paul traveled extensively through the Gentile world, spreading the message of Jesus. The letters of Paul, also known as the "Epistles," are written to many of these communities and contain the fundamental Christian beliefs and instructions on how followers of Christ are to live.

Romans

A very important letter explaining the fundamentals of salvation, the essential matters to Christianity and those of lesser importance. Paul also wrote this letter to strengthen, encourage, and unite the Christians in Rome, imparting wisdom to them regarding proper conduct with each other despite their differing backgrounds.

1 Corinthians

In this letter Paul addresses some serious problems that have crept into the Corinthian congregation, such as division, immorality, marital strife, church discipline, and issues regarding worship.

2 Corinthians

This is a subsequent letter to 1 Corinthians, and in it Paul addresses issues related to his authority as an Apostle, forgiveness, and giving to others.

Galatians

This book addresses the controversy caused by peopled advocating for adherence to the Mosaic Law, especially the practice of circumcision. Paul stresses that salvation is by grace and not by any of the works of the Law.

Ephesians

This letter emphasizes that the followers of Christ are all members of the Body of Christ. It also reiterates the most fundamental doctrines of One Body, One Lord, One God, One Hope, One Faith, One Baptism, and One Spirit, and ends with an encouragement for Christ's followers to stand united in the face of all opposition.

Philippians

Often referred to as "the book of joy" because of the numerous times Jesus' followers are told to have joy and to "rejoice in the Lord." It involves practical instructions on how to live honorably as citizens of heaven, humbly as servants of Christ, and obediently as children of God.

Colossians

Warns the reader to guard against false teachers and heresy, and provides rules for holy living.

1 Thessalonians

Provides specific instructions concerning relationships among Christians, explains the current state and future hope of those who have died, and encouragement to look to the hope of Christ's return for the church.

2 Thessalonians

Paul provides additional encouragement about the coming of Christ for the church, and a call to stay strong in their faith.

- Paul's Pastoral Letters -

The following letters were written by Paul to individuals who had oversight in the church, and they address issues of leadership and doctrine.

1 Timothy

Instructs the reader on how to oppose false teaching and includes instruction on the behavior of the church—especially on how leaders are to behave.

2 Timothy

Exhorts strength and endurance in times of persecution and contains instruction on properly handling Scripture and fulfilling one's personal ministry.

Titus

This letter speaks mostly about morality, good works, and good conduct both in the church and in the world. This was Paul's final letter before he was executed by the Romans.

Philemon

A personal letter from Paul to a man named Philemon regarding a runaway slave, Oneismus. This book sheds light on the shift in social and cultural norms within the Christian circles at the time of Paul.

- Other Letters -

The following letters vary in length and are written by various apostles and leaders in the early church.

Hebrews

This book emphasizes the completion of the old covenant by Jesus' life and death, and encourages the reader not to let their faith be shaken. It shows how Jesus is "better" than what the Jews had under the Law (the word "better" occurs 16 times in the 13 chapters of Hebrews). It also recounts many of the Old Testament "heroes of the faith" who showed great trust in God, and urges the reader to follow their example and endure in holiness. It also expands on Jesus' role and duties as a high priest.

James

By bringing back to remembrance the Old Testament Law, the book of James highlights the importance of doing good works and how genuine faith is demonstrated by obedience. James' focus is not on a believer's salvation, but rather their manner of life. His emphasis is that believers should live their faith. This book also cautions to guard the tongue and seek God's wisdom in all things.

1 Peter
Addresses the suffering experienced by persecuted Christians, and encourages them to stand fast in the living hope.

2 Peter
Warns against false teachers and further impresses upon the reader the importance of right living while awaiting the return of Christ.

1, 2, & 3 John
These books address subjects such as the validity of Christ, Christian conduct and teaching, love, truth, and faithfulness. They also warn against becoming distracted from God-centered living.

Jude
Jude contains a wonderful and poignant message about grace, a warning against apostasy, and a call to uphold and defend the Christian faith.

- End Times -

Revelation
This is a prophetic book written by the Apostle John. It speaks about events in the last days and the final 7-year period of time commonly known as the Great Tribulation, as well as describing the New Jerusalem, a huge and magnificent city with streets of gold.

What is Spirit & Truth Fellowship International®?

Spirit & Truth Fellowship International (STFonline.org) is a ministry that is teaching, training, and networking likeminded Christians around the world who desire to make known the Good News of the Lord Jesus Christ. As a legal entity, we are a non-profit, tax-exempt United States (Indiana) corporation.

Our Vision Statement is: "Building an Enduring Work of Truth." Our vision is demonstrated through various strategies that are anchored in our four core values of truth, integrity, courage, and liberty.

Our Mission Statement is: "To provide sound, biblically-based teaching and training to equip and empower Christians, and to facilitate a network of likeminded individuals, fellowships, and churches."

Spirit & Truth Fellowship International is accomplishing its overall mission by way of live speakers, audio and video teachings, books, seminars, websites, camps and conferences. Our biblically based teachings and networking point people toward an intimate relationship with the Lord Jesus Christ, and are designed to promote personal spiritual growth.

Spirit & Truth Fellowship International has its Home Office in Indiana and assists the networking of fellowships around the world (STFonline.org/churches). Our partners and supporters are Christians who freely affiliate themselves with us because they are in general agreement with our doctrine and practice, and want to be a part of spreading these truths around the world.

Our name is partially derived from Jesus' statement in John 4:23 and 24 that God is seeking people to worship Him "…in spirit and in truth." The basis for all our efforts is the Bible, which we believe to be the Word of God, perfect in its original writing. So-called errors, contradictions, or discrepancies are the result of man's subsequent interference in the translation or transmission of the text, or his failure to understand what is written.

Spirit & Truth Fellowship International draws from all relevant sources that shed light on the integrity of Scripture, such as geography, customs, language, history, and principles governing Bible interpretation. We seek the truth without respect to tradition, "orthodoxy," or popular trends and teachings. Jesus declared himself as the truth, and stated that knowing the truth would set one free. Our vision of "Building an Enduring Work of Truth" is in obedience to Jesus' command to "…go and make disciples of all nations..." (Matt. 28:19).

Any individual willing to examine his beliefs in the light of God's Word can profit from our teachings. They are non-denominational, and are intended to strengthen one's faith in God, Jesus Christ, and the Bible, no matter what his denominational preference may be. Designed primarily for individual home study, the teachings are the result of intensive research and rational methods, making them easy to follow, verify, and practically apply.

If you like what we are doing and you would like to help us continue to spread the Gospel all over the globe, please consider sowing into our ministry at: STFonline.org/donate

CPSIA information can be obtained
at www.ICGtesting.com
Printed in the USA
FSOW03n1548110117
29349FS